BURPS, SCABS and SMELLS

Anita Ganeri

OXFORD
UNIVERSITY PRESS

OXFORD
UNIVERSITY PRESS

Great Clarendon Street, Oxford, OX2 6DP, United Kingdom

Oxford University Press is a department of the University
of Oxford. It furthers the University's objective of excellence
in research, scholarship, and education by publishing
worldwide. Oxford is a registered trade mark of Oxford
University Press in the UK and in certain other countries

Text © Anita Ganeri 2014

British Library Cataloguing in Publication Data
Data available

ISBN: 978-0-19-830820-1

10 9 8 7 6

Paper used in the production of this book is a natural, recyclable product
made from wood grown in sustainable forests. The manufacturing process
conforms to the environmental regulations of the country of origin.

Printed in China by Golden Cup

Acknowledgements

Series Editor: Nikki Gamble

Illustrations by Tony Trimmer
Designed and typeset by Fiona Lee, Pounce Creative

Contents

Is It OK to Pick a Scab?

Hi Dr Sicknote!

I've got a big scab on my knee. Is it OK to pick it?

Hello Emily!

I wouldn't, if I were you. Your scab's really useful.

It works like a bandage, covering your cut until it heals. Here's what happens ...

1. When you cut yourself, special **blood cells** stick together. This is called a clot.

Your scab will fall off when it's ready – probably in a week or two.

If you pick your scab, the cut will take longer to heal and you could end up with a scar.

SO LEAVE IT ALONE!

2. The clot plugs the cut to stop it bleeding.

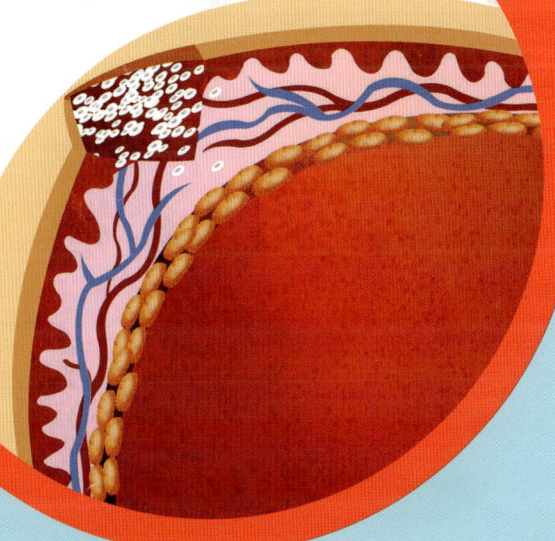

3. After the bleeding stops, the clot becomes dry and crusty. Now it's a scab.

5

Why Are Bogeys Green?

Hi Dr Sicknote.

Why are my bogeys green when I've got a cold?

Hello Dinesh!

This question really gets up my nose.

Bogeys are made inside your nose from slimy stuff called **mucus**. Mucus traps dirt and germs and stops them reaching your lungs.

nose

mucus

Most of the time, mucus is clear. But it can turn green if you've got a cold. This is because it's full of blood cells that have come to fight and kill the germs. These cells have a green colour, which

TURNS YOUR BOGEYS GREEN!

Sick note

Your bogeys are important. They're a sign that your nose is working properly. Remember, everyone has them!

What Makes Me Burp?

Hi Dr Sicknote!

Why do fizzy drinks always make me burp?

Hello Malia!

Fizzy drinks are full of gas – that's what makes them fizzy! When you swallow your drink, it goes down your **oesophagus** (say u-sof-u-gus) into your stomach. Some of the gas gets forced back up. It bursts out of your mouth as a burp.

The same thing can happen if you scoff your food too quickly. Burping is normal and natural. (Tell your parents I said so!) But it's always polite to say, "Excuse me," or cover your mouth with your hand.

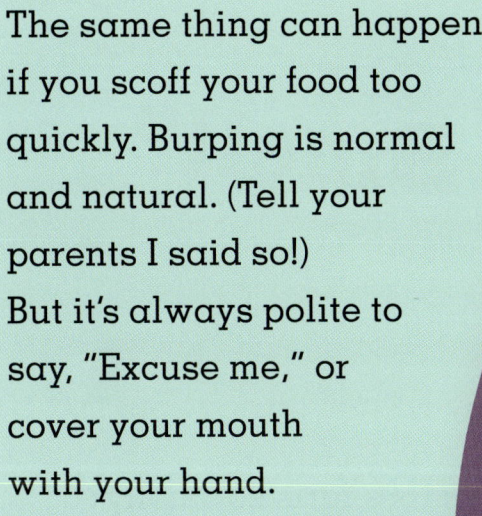

Sick note

The loudest burp on record was noisier than a motorbike – and almost as loud as a chainsaw!

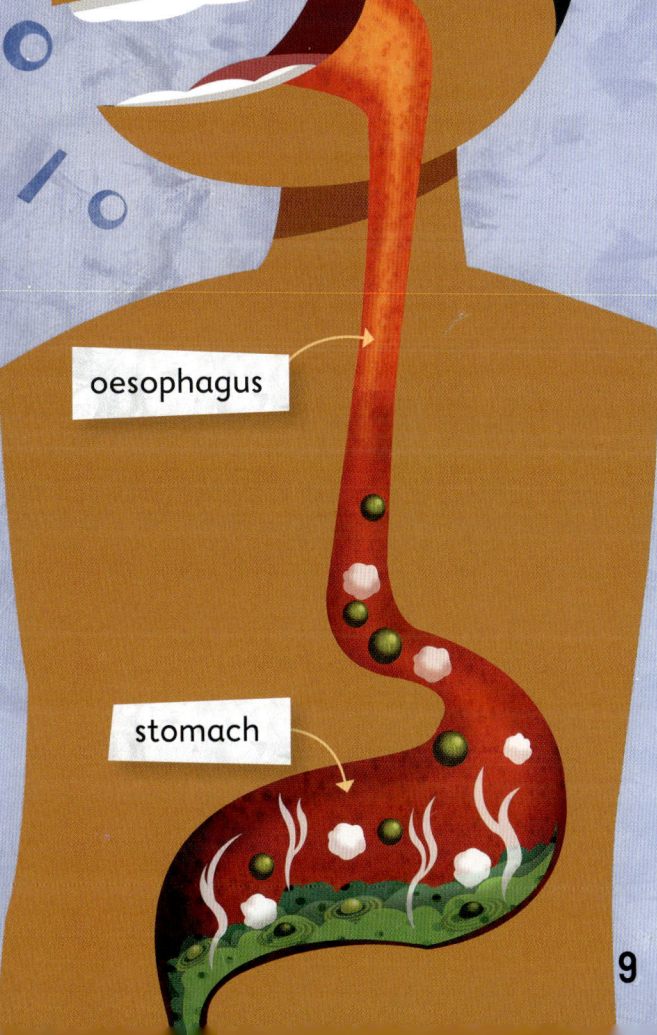

oesophagus

stomach

9

Why Do Farts Smell?

Hi Dr Sicknote.

Why are my sister's farts so smelly?

Hello Seth!

Are you *sure* it's your sister? I usually blame the dog.

Farts work a bit like burps. When you swallow your food, you also gulp down gassy air. As your body gets busy **digesting** your food, it makes more gas.

All that gas has to go somewhere – some of it comes out of your bottom!

Some farts are loud and don't smell. Others are silent, but super-stinky! That's because they're full of really smelly gases. Most people fart around 14 times a day – including your sister!

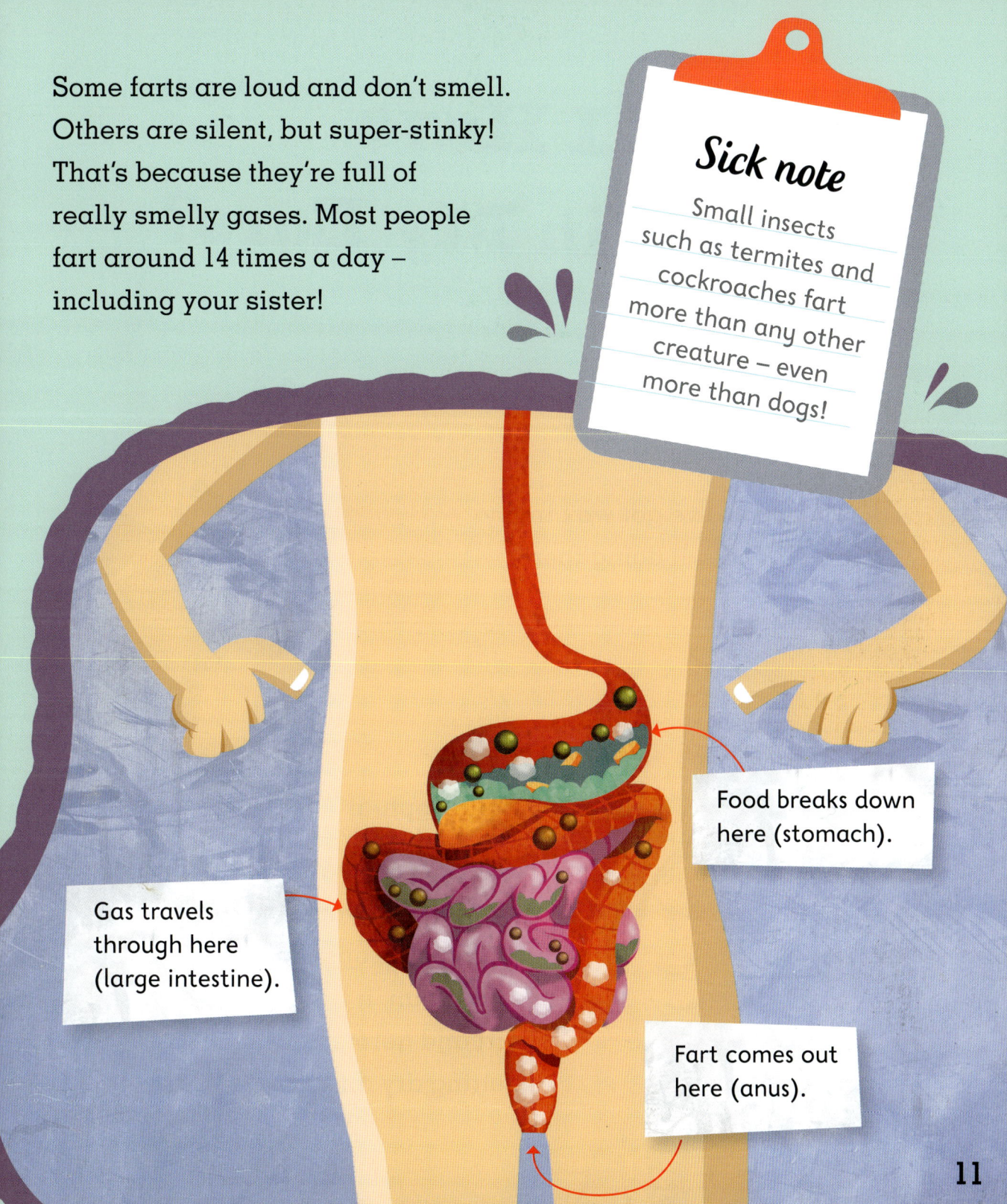

Sick note

Small insects such as termites and cockroaches fart more than any other creature – even more than dogs!

Food breaks down here (stomach).

Gas travels through here (large intestine).

Fart comes out here (anus).

Why Do I Have Wax in My Ears?

Hi Dr Sicknote.

Mum says I've got wax in my ears. What's it doing there?

Hello Sophia!

You do have wax in your ears – earwax! Earwax is squishy yellow stuff that keeps the insides of your ears clean. It traps harmful dust, dirt and germs, and stops your ears getting dry and itchy.

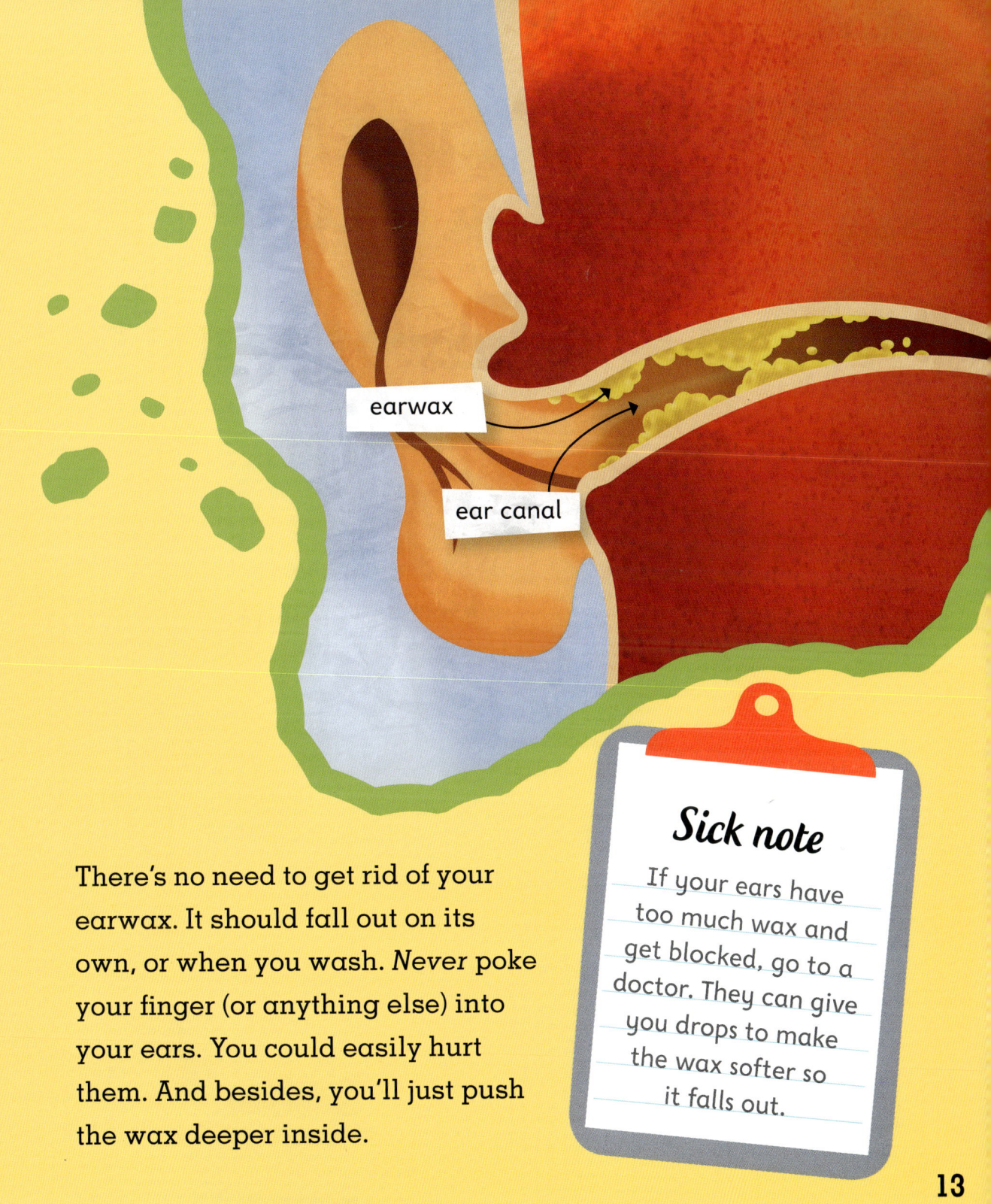

earwax

ear canal

There's no need to get rid of your earwax. It should fall out on its own, or when you wash. *Never poke your finger (or anything else) into your ears.* You could easily hurt them. And besides, you'll just push the wax deeper inside.

Sick note

If your ears have too much wax and get blocked, go to a doctor. They can give you drops to make the wax softer so it falls out.

Why Does  Sick Have Carrots in It?

Hi Dr Sicknote.

Why does my sick always have carrots in it? I *hate* carrots!

Hello Sebastian!

It's strange, isn't it? You get that funny feeling in your tummy and before you know it, you've thrown up your dinner. And **vomit** usually looks like it's full of chopped-up carrots. But these are actually bits of all different foods that have been mixed up with your stomach juices.

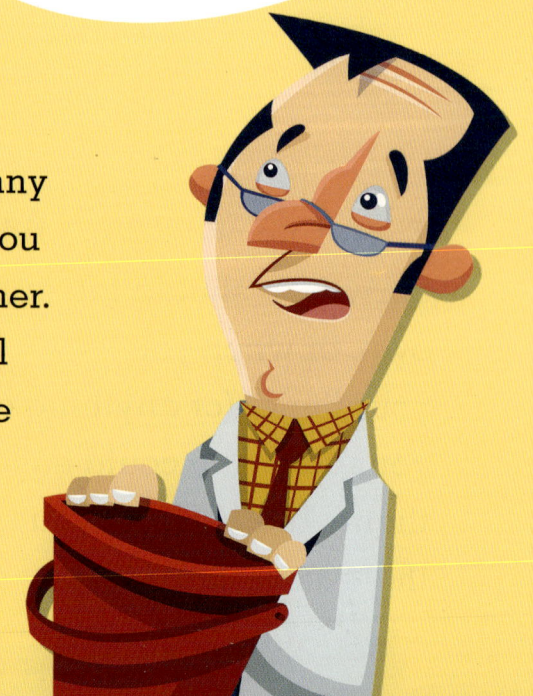

3. The food comes out of the mouth as vomit.

2. This causes food to travel back up the oesophagus.

You see, throwing up is your body's way of getting rid of something nasty. Your stomach muscles squeeze until they've pushed your half-eaten food back up your throat and out of your mouth.

Sometimes you throw up because of germs in your tummy. Sometimes it's because you've eaten too fast or the food was bad.

Start here.

1. The stomach muscles squeeze, pushing food upwards.

Why Am I Covered in Spots?

Hi Dr Sicknote.

Help! I'm covered in spots!
What's wrong with me?

Hello Lien!

Have you got a runny nose and a cough, too? If so, you've probably got chickenpox.

Some people only get a few spots when they have chickenpox. Others get spots all over – even in their mouth and ears!

1. Spots start to appear on the skin.

2. After a while, the spots form blisters.

3. Finally, the blisters dry up and go crusty.

After a few days, your spots will go crusty. They will probably itch *a lot*. I know it's hard but try not to scratch them. If you do, germs might get in, or the spots might leave a scar.

Chickenpox is easy to spread, too, so you should stay away from school until the scabs fall off. (See, it's not all bad news!)

Sick note

Nobody is sure how chickenpox got its name. It might be because the spots look like you've been pecked by a chicken!

How Can You Stop Hiccups?

HIC! CUP!

HIC! CUP!

Hi Dr Sicknote.

I've – *hiccup!* – got hiccups. How – *hiccup!* – can I make them – *hiccup!* – stop?

Hello Isaac!

Sometimes a fright helps.

BOO!

Did that work? If not, try drinking water from the wrong side of a glass, or holding your breath and counting to ten.

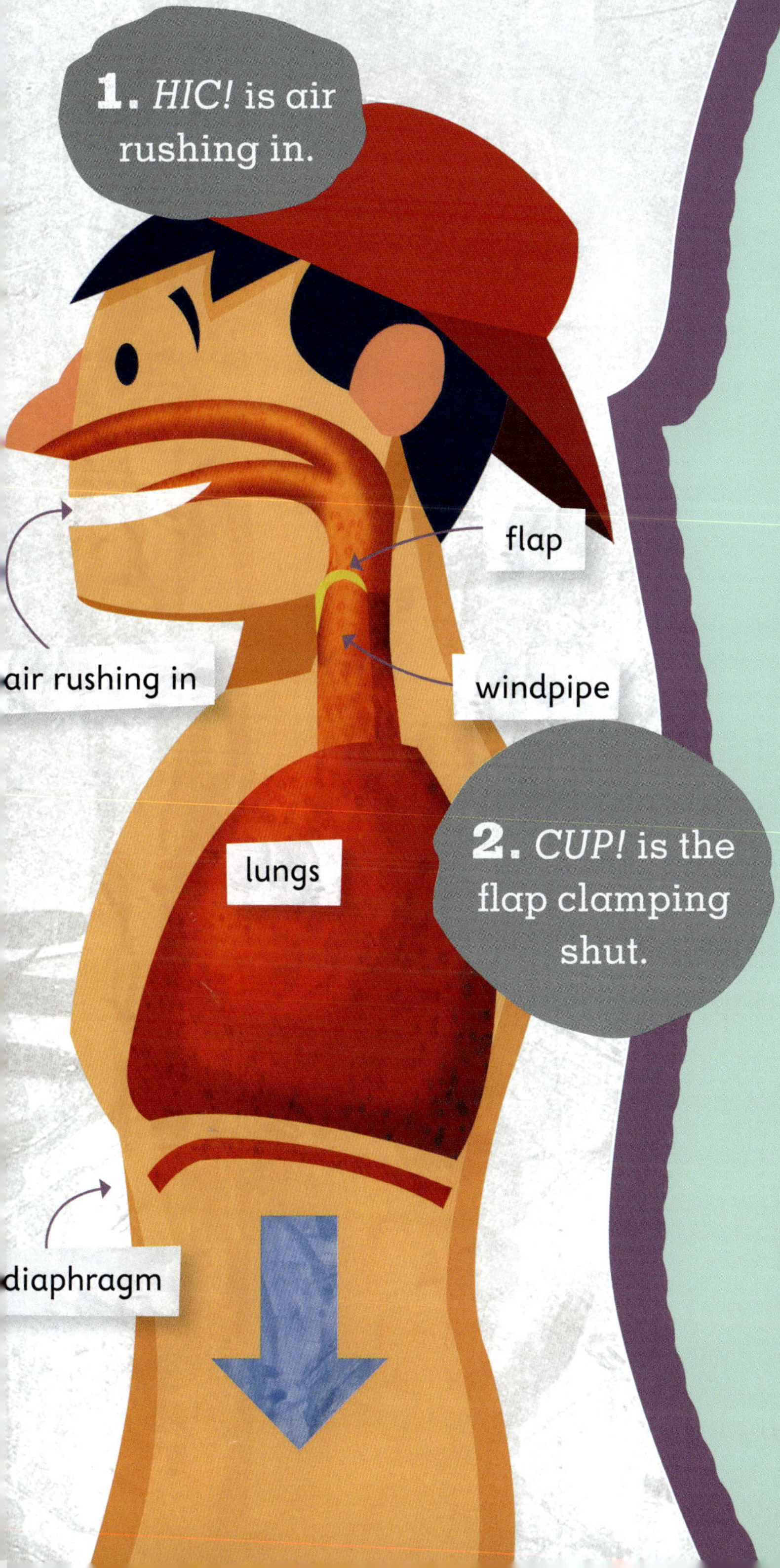

1. *HIC!* is air rushing in.

flap

air rushing in

windpipe

lungs

2. *CUP!* is the flap clamping shut.

diaphragm

Hiccups happen when your **diaphragm** (*say* digh-u-fram) suddenly pulls down really hard, forcing you to suck in lots of air. To stop all that air rushing into your lungs, a flap at the top of your windpipe snaps shut, making a hiccuping sound!

Sick note

A man called Charles Osborne had the longest attack of hiccups ever recorded. His hiccups lasted for 68 years!

Why Do I Keep Yawning?

Hi Dr Sicknote.

Why do I always yawn as soon as I wake up?

Hello Kiera!

That's a good question! Nobody knows for sure but there are lots of ideas.

Some people think that yawning is a way of helping your body wake up. When you yawn, you take in a big gulp of air. It's like a big stretch – for your lungs!

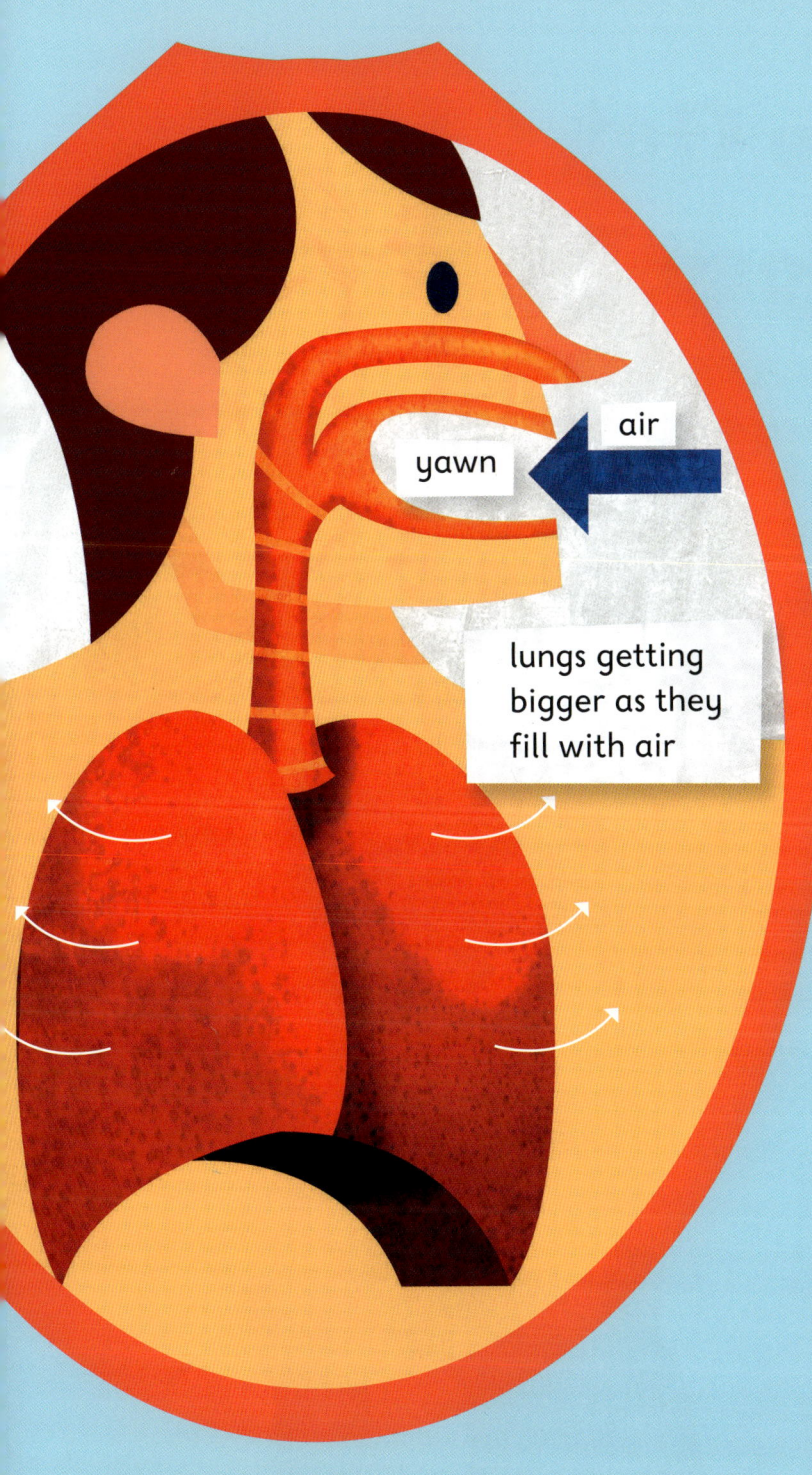

air

yawn

lungs getting bigger as they fill with air

One thing's for sure – yawning is **contagious**. If you see someone yawning, I bet you start yawning, too. You just can't help it. Sometimes just *thinking* about yawning can set you off!

Sick note

Everybody yawns – even babies in their mothers' tummies! Most people yawn around 240 000 times in their life. Each yawn lasts around six seconds.

Do Geese Get Goose Bumps?

Hi Dr Sicknote.

When I'm c-c-cold, I always get goose bumps.

Do g-g-geese get them, too?

Hello Jerome!

No, they don't because they don't have furry or hairy skin! They have feathers.

Your hairs stand on end because they're trying to keep you warm. This doesn't work very well, though, because you're not hairy enough!

Goose bumps were more useful long ago, when humans were much hairier.

Sick note

Goose bumps got their name because they make your skin look like the knobbly skin of a goose that has been plucked for cooking. Yikes!

Here's how goose bumps happen:

1. When you get cold, the hairs on your body try to stand on end.

2. Each hair is attached to a tiny muscle that pulls it up.

3. The muscle also pulls up a tiny bump of skin, which we call a goose bump.

Glossary

blood cells: tiny parts that are in your blood

contagious: easily passed on to other people

diaphragm: a flat muscle in your chest, underneath your lungs

digesting: breaking down your food into tiny pieces that can be used to help your body work

germs: tiny living things that can cause you to get ill

mucus: slippery material that lines your nose, lungs and stomach

oesophagus: the tube that carries food from your mouth to your stomach

vomit: food that has come back up from the stomach to the mouth

Index